The Soul Sister Rising

Verses for the Women Who Rise : From
wounds to wings

Nidhi Anthwal [Shreem]

India | USA | UK

Made with ❤ on the BookLeaf Publishing Platform
www.bookleafpub.in
www.bookleafpub.com

Dedication

To the Fierce and Eternal Divine Within.

Preface

There comes a time in every woman's life when she must choose herself. This book is born from that choice, the choice to rise and to turn the cracks into constellations.

The Soul Sister Rising is not just a collection of words; it is a sanctuary for every woman who has loved, lost, longed, and learned. It is for the ones who have held their breath in heartbreak, who have dimmed their light to fit into spaces never meant for them, who have whispered their dreams into the night, wondering if the universe was listening. Yes, the universe was listening. It always was.

This book is for the dreamers, the healers, the givers, the warriors. May these pages remind you that your heart is not too heavy and your love is not too wild.

I hope within these words, you will find your way home.

With love,
Nidhi Anthwal [Shreem]

Acknowledgements

I am deeply grateful to the divine for guiding me through this journey and giving me the strength to bring this book to life. To my family, your love and unwavering support have been my greatest blessing.

And to you, dear reader, I hope these pages hold you and remind you of the fire in your heart, the ocean in your soul, and the universe within you. You are your own rising.

Wearing time like a celestial crown

I wasn't ready to grow up,
clinging to dreams that fluttered like fireflies
But here I stand now
bathed in the soft glow of my youth
The bold lipsticks I wore as a child, once playful and
carefree
now blend with my age, creating a harmony that only
time can weave.

My long hair, woven with memories,
falls like the pages of stories I am still writing,
each strand carrying echoes of the past,
whispers of the girl I once was.

I cherish the old, the out-of-style treasures that hold so
much soul,
like my mother's dark purple lipstick, a shade with
warmth of her laughter.
The gossip of aunts wraps around me,
a thread connecting the past to now.
The men I once saw as uncles
now glance at me differently,
it's a strange shift, but I'm not bothered

and do not shrink from.
I have learned to sit in my own light,
unapologetic, steady.

Nothing breaks my heart anymore.
I have softened, but not weakened,
like pages worn from a cherished book being read too
many times.
I find peace in the slow things
the weight of a book in my hands,
the hush of a room before sunrise,
the quiet luxury of choosing myself.

I do not cut my hair for nothing.
It grows with me, a timeline I refuse to erase.
The girl who once wanted to be seen
now finds joy in being know
by herself, by the universe,
by the warmth of a life unfolding exactly as it should.

I wasn't ready to grow up,
but here I stand,
draped in the glow of my own becoming,
wearing time like a celestial crown.

The Queen's Code

Red is not your color until the world decides you've
earned it.
And even then, red should be soft, subdued, never
daring, never loud.
I have burned in silence,
dimmed my fire to fit in spaces
never meant for me.
I was told to be strong enough to wait,
but not to change.
my desires are shadows and fleeting
Hold them gently like whispers, but never too near.

You can dream, but don't reach.
Be a go-getter, but expect to stay.
Want, but not too much.
They tell you to be loved, you must shrink.
But I do not wait to be chosen.
A storm rose within me
And I will not apologize for it.
I build my own throne,
a seat carved from all they feared in me.
And I sit upon it.
Unapologetic. Unshaken. Unafraid.
They want me moldable, manageable, quiet.

I refuse because I crack the queen's code.

They cradle flames only when they flicker,
never when they rage.
But I was never meant to be tamed.
I do not hush. I do not smolder.
I do not wait.
I ignite. I burn.

A Prayer for Freedom

To whom she replaced me in her heart
She said I was Hers and now I'm lost
If all this time was a fiction
And the plot changed overnight
Yet I desire her touch eternally
No matter whichever form it takes
Day by day it's icier and more on the surface
That can only shatter me till the atom of my soul
Her words beautifully fierce
Possibly bold
Not to worry I'm losing my own voice
Cause I know love comes with a price
Oh lord I won't lie
When I say I love her with my life
And the only thing I'd hate from her
Is the kiss that says goodbye.

Poetry is for those who lack the courage

I don't read and write cute poetry
when it can be cruel
When it knows the pain we cherish,
pressing into the wounds we refuse to heal,
replaying the most memorable ache.
Poetry is for those who lack the courage
to put an end to everything
a key to slip beyond the prison of flesh and bone,
a window into the world beyond suffering.
It is the knife we stare into,
seeing our reflection in its edge,
watching life carve its scars upon us.
It is the story of the unfortunate,
where tears are shed in silence,
the soul's quiet passion to escape the plane,
the whispered dream of life unchained.

Face it

I know you hate me because I was the sacred mirror,
reflecting the wounds you needed to heal within
yourself.
My presence in your life exposed all your shadows to the
light,
making you believe I was the source of your
unhappiness,
when in truth, I was guided by the soul and the ultimate
love of the divine.
I tried to weave your broken heart with the threads of
faith,
but your ego strangled me in the barbed wires of
incomprehension.
I should've known the scariest thing for you was to face
your true self.
Meet me when you've finally met you.

Whatever Lies In Between

A mutual realization
we are not in love,
but we still ache for whatever exists in between.
A burden of hurt or lust
something we carry but never claim.
We rush to get the dirt off,
only to backpedal deeper into the mud.
We count the days like we count the stars,
losing track of where we began.
We promise a summer together,
knowing well we both despise the sun.
We fear the fire will burn out,
yet we are nothing but smoke in the air.

Unbound

For me, love has no lines
no borders between a god, a friend, a lover,
an animal, or even a passing shadow.
My heart cradles the essence,
the quiet hum beneath it all.
The spirit caged within my bones
reaches for warmth,
flows with the echo of a soul,
flies for the freedom
never bound to the surface,
never confined to the vessel.

The absence of life

You never learned how to live,
so you set fire to the moments in between.
Once the smoke curls through your mind,
there is no difference between escape and entrapment
just a slow unraveling of what once was.

The flame catches,
your soul thinning into ashes on the floor.
Each drag, a silent failure,
each exhale, a lesson in losing yourself.
You smoked away your fears
until you became one.

Every cigarette crushed under your boot was
extinguished
by the weight of something precious you couldn't carry.
You didn't breathe the absence of life
but the loss of it.

The heart unowned

Why is my heart the way it is.
How can I put everything it feels in words
It is strange it's mine but I can not understand
I need someone else to say what it can't
It shivers with hate and love as if there's no difference
It wants to fly and fall at the same time same space '
Like hot red rose it blushes and
Like cool blue fire it burns
It longs to stay young but cries to get settled
It craves connection yet tries to escape
It throbs as if music is flowing through me
If only I could know the lyrics it would be at ease
I wish to give it to you but it's inside me
Looks like it knows who's it is
Still it wanders every second like lost star
What it is whispering to me about you
Who poured this secret language inside it
Why only answers in it are questions
It cares for all but is careless for the owner
As If it is someone else's life living inside of me.

The breath I lost

I am drowning in my own tears,
I see no shore to rescue.
All these nights I stay awake
wishing the dreams I build were not to lie in the ruins.
I'm not sure how I'll survive
My delightful dreams being broken beyond repair.
All I know is I'm morphed into a hollow shell
I've lost too much weight of my being
Only to drag it in my soul.
I've poured my heartache over hundreds of pages
But my barren words refused to heal me.
Every day is a battle to remind myself who I was
But from a shadow all a distant memory.
My very essence is flickering,
My chemistry irrevocably altered
Still I write not in any hope of reconciliation
But to release from the chains of hopeless resentment
that binds me
So I can reclaim breathing as recovery.

My love isn't a sprint

Wait.
Because my love isn't a sprint.
My is the slow burn of a candle in a dim-lit room,
body swaying gently, until the wax drips and carves a
story in its fall.
My love is breathing slowly,
till I hear my heart beating in my ears.
My love is sipping on my favorite cup of coffee,
wrapped in the softness of an early morning bed.
My love is reading a book,
highlighting all the beautiful lines,
saving them for moments that matter.
My love is walking on petals of roses,
smelling like one.
My love is watching my comfort movie,
falling asleep in between,
but waking up just to replay the parts I missed.
And I fear
I cannot give it to you in a rush to race.
But I see you're in a hurry,
so go before you learn what it is to stay.

Tides of an empty touch

I sit on the shore,
memories of our love come like a gentle wave,
kissing my toes
then the frigidity of the past quickly travels to my heart.
I look up at the sky, then at the sea,
then down at my scars, blue as ever,
and I remember chasing that bruised blue forever.
It takes me a little longer to exhale,
a tough effort to breathe more,
so I stay lifeless,
with only air gently embracing me.
I throw a stone into the calm water,
and it feels like I've thrown myself.
I feel the icy water warm against my frozen flesh,
holding me with all the ripples and turbulences I've
caused,
as if it were an imaginary lover,
clinging to me in longing,
whispering through each wave,
'I will not let you go.' "
Then I try to catch it with my hand,
but there's only sand that flows through my fingers,
and I feel so empty-handed.
The only thing I wished for

was that emptiness could take shape
and fill the spaces between my fingers.

15

Love spells

You don't have any idea, do you?
How much it hurts my heart
When you leave the room unaware
That I'm having a full heart-to-heart
With you in my head, words echoing,
Hitting the walls of my brain,
But my tongue won't say a thing.
I gaze at your back as you walk away,
And my mind goes blank again.
Because of you, my heart is a mess,
A puzzle I don't wish to solve.

I love how these boundless nights
Give me time to be lost in your thoughts.
And somewhere on this earth,
I know you are searching for me.
I want you to know it works
My heart is longing for you.
This is fate, isn't it?
You and me, so distant, yet meant to be.
So together, we compose a love song
Perfect for our lips.
And on days when lyrics drift,
We find them in our kiss.

From my love blinded eyes,
How hopeless I am to see the flaws
That others saw in you,
The ones they warned me about.
I beg you, show me your weapons,
Tell me how you are killing me
With the softest thing in the world called love
I wish I could be like them,
Unaffected, untouched,
when you impair me.
What spell have you cast on me?
Even in my dreams,
Unloving you is a question
Beyond my existence.
You showed me love for a moment,
And that moment became my whole life.

I sincerely wish we could embrace our own souls,
But I know it's hardly a question.
So my soul has found yours,
To hold you in this lifetime and the great beyond.
To love every piece that hurts you,
Even the ones that hurt me too.
To keep you close,
Because I know this is my strength.
To throw myself entirely into you,

To surrender to the ache,
Knowing I would be lost in nothingness without the
pain.

The abyss

I was holding on by a thread,
fragile, desperate,
between survival and the abyss.
My shirt was hooked,
a single strand of hair caught on the metal edge,
the last delicate tether between me and the fall.
And you could have reached out,
could have pulled me up.
But instead, you reached for what had been hidden all
along
the knife, the sharp betrayal I never saw coming.
With a single, merciless snip,
you severed that fragile strand,
tore my shirt,
and let the fabric rip like the last remnants of hope.
The rope that held me was gone.
and God, I fell.
Harder than I ever imagined,
deeper than I ever feared.
But you stood there, watching.
As if it was inevitable,
as if this was always meant to be.
And then, with the coldest finality, you said it
the girl gone bad for you.

But I was never good enough to begin with, was I?
When I fell, the impact never came
not in the way it should have,
not in the way one expects when crashing down from so
high.
There was no sharp sting, no gasp of agony,
no desperate reaching for solid ground.
The world around me turned silent, distant,
The stones, the thorns, the shards of glass
tore through me,
painted my white shirt red,
carved through fabric and skin alike,
but I did not flinch.
I didn't know if I was still there,
if I was still real,
if I was still someone at all.
But I saw the abyss,
and in that quiet, infinite void,
the abyss saw me too.

Rebuild

I shouldn't have let you slip away like water through my
fingers.
Shouldn't have let you grow on me like ivy,
twisting, tightening and suffocating the essence of me.
I was a girl, but I always had this woman inside me,
A tigress waiting, claws sheathed, fire caged.
I could have pounced, could have torn mountains down,
could have let the earth tremble beneath my wrath.
But the conditioning became your shield.
I was big, yet I shrank.
I held integrity, yet I folded.
You tore through my childlike heart,
ripped innocence at the seams,
left me bleeding poetry onto pages
that refused to heal me..
Every pulse in my body screams,
Rebuild. Rise.
From the glass ruins where no piece of me remains,
I carve something new, something untouchable.
I won't turn back to ashes
Won't waste breath naming ghosts.
Won't flinch at the memory of who held the knife.
She is done. She is gone.
And in her place,

A woman who rolls her eyes and walks with such power,
even her earrings leave battle scars
as they kiss her skin.
A force burning gold and red,
Mother of Divine, one with her soul.
No line she won't cross to build herself
So she can return stronger.
Because someone like her?
She was never killed.
She was only reborn.

Crowned in divinity

The silence was not stillness.
It was the gathering of storms.
Finally she stood up
Rivers of fire running down her cheeks
The truth scorched its way through her
Grief pressed against her chest like a tombstone,
But her heartbeat pounded like war drums,
A rhythm reminding her that she was still here,
Owning air that fills her lungs.
Her suffering transformed into divine purification
She has become the woman
She was always meant to be
She stands tall
wrapped in her own fire
life does not happen *to* her
it bends at her will,
it bows to the woman who walked through the fire
and emerged crowned in divinity.

Intuition

The knowing settles in her bones like an ache.
The weak strip her of her true power
the power of deep knowing,
of flowing effortlessly in her feminine essence.
They deceive her into carrying burdens that were never
hers,
twisting the soft fabric of her soul into something brittle,
something wounded.
But a woman woven with magic cannot be fooled.
The wind murmurs its truths,
the bees hum their warnings,
the butterflies shudder before the storm arrives.
She breathes in her own power
before offering her air to another.
And that is why the weak fear her.
They mask it as mockery,
as dismissal,
because her knowing is an untamed thing.
She moves now with the weight of the ocean in her
veins,
With the knowing of the stars in her breath.
Her intuition is her birthright
Because a woman who listens to her own voice?
She cannot be fooled.

She cannot be controlled.
She is the divine.

25

Dreams

I sit on the shore,
memories of our love come like a gentle wave,
kissing my toes
then the frigidity of the past quickly travels to my heart.
I look up at the sky, then at the sea,
then down at my scars, blue as ever,
and I remember chasing that bruised blue forever.
It takes me a little longer to exhale,
a tough effort to breathe more,
so I stay lifeless,
with only air gently embracing me.
I throw a stone into the calm water,
and it feels like I've thrown myself.
I feel the icy water warm against my frozen flesh,
holding me with all the ripples and turbulences I've
caused,
as if it were an imaginary lover,
clinging to me in longing,
whispering through each wave,
'I will not let you go.' "
Then I try to catch it with my hand,
but there's only sand that flows through my fingers,
and I feel so empty-handed.
The only thing I wished for

was that emptiness could take shape
and fill the spaces between my fingers.

Prophecy

She does not chase. She remembers.
She does not yearn. She reclaims.
For before this moment, before even the first breath of
longing
She was already written into the stars.
The hands that once trembled now trace poetry into the
wind.
She doesn't wonder if she belongs. She already does
She was carved from the same fire as the sun.
Her desire is divine. Her longing is prophecy. That
hunger is holy.
She stands at the gates of destiny as its rightful heir.
Let the sky bear witness to her awakening.

She was, and had always always been, her own

The ache of a life half-lived beneath the gaze of others,
The slow erosion of self
It would not have shouted;
it would have whispered,
in the way a woman looks at her reflection not to admire
but to remember that she exists beyond the roles she
plays.
She was, and had always been, her own.
In the quiet before dawn
When the world is still
She remembers,
even for a moment,
that she belongs not to duty,
nor to expectation,
nor to the hands that hold her
but to herself.
a sky meant to stretch endlessly
a song that longed to be sung,
a fire told to be only warmth.
Maybe she would only take one step.
But that step would be hers, hers alone.
She is the breath before sound,
the spark before fire

She is love and devotion

and she was, and had always been, her own.

Who will you be

There is a weight we do not name,
a burden we do not recognize
We wake in the morning and do not know who we are
until duty calls our name,
until the world places upon us a task, a sorrow, a mouth
to feed, a wound to tend.
And in the bending of our backs beneath the weight of
another's grief, another's hunger, another's silent plea,
we whisper: *Ah, here I am. This is who I am*
we walk through life as a collection of reflections,
the shape we take in the presence of others just like how
water takes shape of the vessel
you are good when you are a giver,
but what will they say when your hands are empty?
Who will you be then?
A healer, a lover, a quiet pillar of solace
do these names really belong to us
Are we just the echoes of praise or the absence of it
will we dissolve into nothingness without them?